Mountain Emerald

Dragonflies
of
Alaska

John Hudson
and
Robert H. Armstrong

Text © John Hudson & Robert H. Armstrong

Photographs © Robert H. Armstrong, except: p. 11 (top), Richard Carstensen; pp. 14 & 17, Cameron Eckert; p. 28, Oleg Kosterin; p. 41, Ray Bruun; p. 46 (top & middle), Dennis Paulson; p. 46 (bottom), Ian Lane.

Illustrations by Robert A. Cannings, © Royal British Columbia Museum, except American Emerald illustrations by Dominic Chaloner.

Cover: Alaska's State Insect, the Four-spotted Skimmer dragonfly

Copies of this book may be purchased through Todd Communications, 203 W. 15th Ave., Suite 102, Anchorage, AK 99501 USA. Phone: (907) 274-8633

Printed by Everbest Printing Co., Ltd., China
First Printing, May 2005
10 9 8 7 6 5 4 3 2 1

ISBN: 1-57833-302-4
Library of Congress Control Number: 2005903576

2

Contents

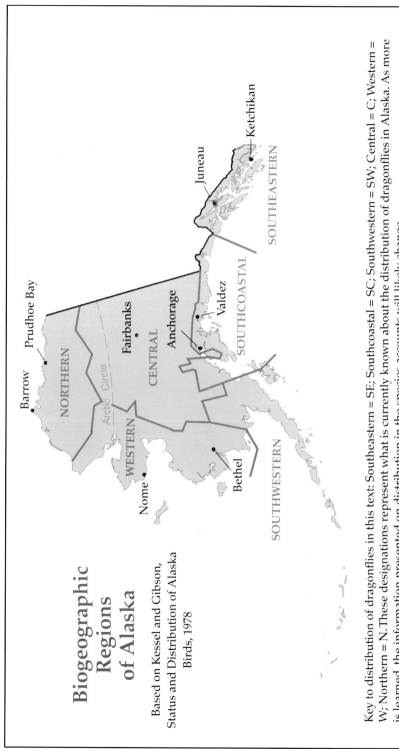

Biogeographic Regions of Alaska

Based on Kessel and Gibson, Status and Distribution of Alaska Birds, 1978

NORTHERN

WESTERN

CENTRAL

SOUTHWESTERN

SOUTHCOASTAL

SOUTHEASTERN

Arctic Circle

Barrow

Prudhoe Bay

Nome

Fairbanks

Bethel

Anchorage

Valdez

Juneau

Ketchikan

Key to distribution of dragonflies in this text: Southeastern = SE; Southcoastal = SC; Southwestern = SW; Central = C; Western = W; Northern = N. These designations represent what is currently known about the distribution of dragonflies in Alaska. As more is learned, the information presented on distribution in the species accounts will likely change.

Dragonflies in Alaska

Alaska may be best known for its salmon, bears, and whales, but the 49th State is also home to more than 30 species of dragonflies. Dragonflies cruise Alaska's summer skies from Ketchikan to north of the Brooks Range and from the Alaska Peninsula to the Yukon border. While our small number of species pales in comparison to that of every other state (Florida, for example, has 170 species), anyone interested in these beautiful insects can use this guide to identify most of our species.

Many dragonflies found in Alaska have common or scientific names related to the state's geographic location. Alaska is "northern," and much of the state is boreal or subarctic, so one should not be surprised it is home to the Northern Bluet, Northern Spreadwing, Boreal Bluet, Boreal Whiteface, Subarctic Darner, Subarctic Bluet and Taiga Bluet. The species name for Azure Darner is *septentrionalis*, meaning "of the north," and *sitchensis*, the species name for the Zigzag Darner, means Sitka in honor of the Alaska city where the original specimen was collected and described for science.

Watching Alaska's Dragonflies

Watching Alaska's dragonflies can be fun and educational. Their large size and habit of concentrating along the shores of ponds, lakes and marshes make them easy to observe. Armed with a pair of close-focusing binoculars, a little patience, and a dry place to sit you can see many fascinating aspects of their behavior. Watch their incredible flight patterns and how easily they outmaneuver and capture other insects. Think about their ability to capture around 300 insects, including mosquitoes, a day.

Many of their mating habits can also be observed—males chasing and capturing females, pairs flying in tandem, and the actual mating process when they are in the wheel position. Watch females lay their eggs and think about the habitats that the different species choose.

One of the most exciting facets of dragonfly life history is their emergence from the larval exoskeleton. The whole process from larva to winged adult can be observed at close range.

In the following pages we illustrate and discuss most of the common aspects of dragonfly behavior that you can easily observe.

FLIGHT–When it comes to catching prey, it would appear the adult dragonfly has no limitations. Two large eyes comprised of thousands of facets detect prey in nearly every direction, and four independently con-

Paddle-tailed Darner

trolled wings allow dragonflies to hover, glide, and move in any direction. Some species are able to fly 35 mph. The six spine-covered legs can extend to form a basket to catch prey. The prey is then transferred to the mouth where sharp-toothed mandibles reduce it to bits.

MATING–Before mating the male seizes the female on or behind the head with clamp-like terminal appendages at the tip of his abdomen. He then flies off with her in tow, much like a truck pulling a trailer. This is the **tandem position** that many people get excited about observing.

While in tandem with the female or just before, the male transfers a sperm packet from the tip of his abdomen to secondary genitalia behind the thorax. Next, the female bends her abdomen down and forward to engage and lock into the male's genitalia. Joined in this way, the pair are said to be in the **wheel position.**

EGG LAYING–Females lay eggs either in tandem with the male or when they are alone. Female Skimmer and Emerald dragonflies release eggs from the tip of the abdomen through a trap door-like structure called the **vulvar lamina.**

The **Four-spotted Skimmer** lays eggs by dipping her abdomen into the water. This species may hold the record for the number of eggs laid at once – over 3300 eggs in a single clutch. Other species flick eggs into water or wet moss while hovering, or tap the abdomen onto wet moss or mud.

Damselflies and Darners, such as this **Subarctic Darner,** insert eggs inside the tissues of aquatic plants or dead wood using a structure near the tip of the abdomen called an ovipositor. The cryptic coloration of this female helps her blend into vegetation to avoid detection.

Northern Spreadwings and other damselflies often lay eggs while in tandem with the male. The keen-eyed and patient observer can find ovipositing females grasping vegetation, the abdomen arched and probing in search of the perfect spot, above or below the water, to deposit her eggs.

LARVAE–Like all insects, dragonflies have both an adult and larval form; however, the casual observer rarely sees the underwater world where larval dragonflies lurk. Larvae possess a hinged lower lip, or **labium,** that folds under the head. When prey are within striking distance, the larvae extend the labium at lightning speed, grasping the target with hooks or teeth. True dragonfly larvae also use a form of jet propulsion to approach swimming prey such as fish. They accomplish this by squirting water from the end of their abdomen.

EMERGENCE—The larval dragonfly lives for months or even years before leaving the water to emerge as the winged insect most people are familiar with.

American Emerald

A dragonfly emerging from its larval exoskeleton is exciting to watch. The entire process from start to finish may take less than an hour. Emergence begins as pressure within splits open the larval skin. After hanging upside-down for a bit, the insect bends forward and grasps the old skin or the perch and pulls its abdomen free.

Next it pumps blood into the veins of its wings, causing them to expand until they are shiny and taut. Then, the blood drains to the abdomen, causing it to elongate. Within a couple of hours the body hardens and the dragonfly flies away.

American Emerald

Hudsonian Whiteface

After emergence, young dragonflies need some time to dry their newly inflated wings. Even after their wings are dry they are very weak flyers for at least most of that day. These newly transformed youngsters are easily recognized by their bright and shiny wings. At this stage they are called **tenerals.**

Damselflies typically crawl out of their larval exoskeleton in a forward position. They may do this on top of lily pads, where several may gather at once. To observe this, try visiting ponds early in the morning, as the juveniles quickly disperse and the larval skins are scavenged.

PREDATORS— During or shortly after emergence, dragonflies are quite vulnerable to capture by birds such as this American Robin. In Alaska, adult dragonflies appear to be important food for American Kestrels, Merlins and Bohemian Waxwings.

This **water strider** is using tube-shaped mouthparts to suck the fluids from a Northern Spreadwing that has drowned in a pond.

Hudsonian Whiteface

Dragonflies may get stuck to the leaves of **carnivorous sundew** plants, which may line the shorelines of bog ponds. The sound of vibrating wings near a sundew patch often signals the presence of a trapped dragonfly.

Identifying Alaska's Dragonflies

Dragonflies belong to the insect order Odonata. The **true dragonflies,** suborder Anisoptera, hold their wings spread horizontally when at rest, and in species found in Alaska, the eyes are connected at the top of the head.

Damselflies, suborder Zygoptera, have widely spaced eyes, and hold their wings together above the body, or partly open as in the Spreadwings, when at rest.

Parts of a Dragonfly

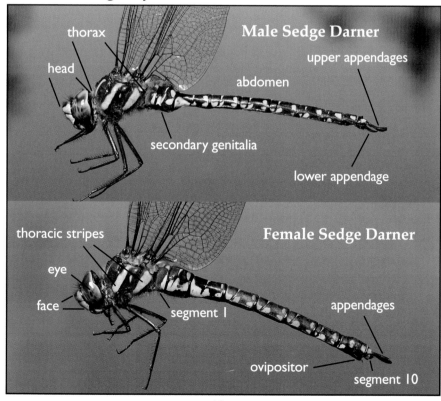

Male Sedge Darner

thorax
head
upper appendages
abdomen
secondary genitalia
lower appendage

Female Sedge Darner

thoracic stripes
eye
face
segment 1
appendages
ovipositor
segment 10

The Damselflies (Suborder Zygoptera)
Spreadwings, Sprites, and Bluets

True to their name, damselflies are delicate insects. Compared to the true dragonflies, their flight is slow and weak and they rarely venture far from shoreline vegetation. Prey are captured either in mid-air on short flights from perches or gleaned from vegetation while flying. Damselflies hold their wings closed over the body or partly open (as in the Spreadwings) when at

rest, and the eyes do not touch in the middle of the head as in true dragonflies. Females deposit eggs inside plant tissues.

Seven damselfly species are currently known from Alaska. Three species, the Northern and Emerald spreadwings (Family Lestidae) and the tiny Sedge Sprite (Family Coenagrionidae) can be readily distinguished by color patterns and by the shape of the male terminal appendages and length of the female ovipositor.

In contrast, identifying our four Bluets (Family Coenagrionidae) can be challenging. All four species are similar in size and color. Look for a black U-shaped mark on top of the second abdominal segment (male Taiga Bluet) or conspicuous black markings on the underside of the thorax (Subarctic Bluet).

If it is not one of these species and it is a male (Males have four appendages at the tip of the abdomen and lack an ovipositor), examine the terminal appendages from the side with a 16X hand lens and the sky or other bright object in the background. The upper appendage of male Northern Bluets is slightly upturned whereas it is rounded in Boreal Bluets.

Emerald Spreadwing
Lestes dryas

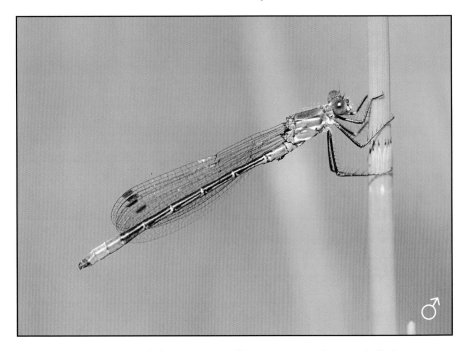

In both sexes, top of thorax metallic green and top of abdomen dark green. In older males, bottom of thorax and abdominal segments 1-2 and 8-10 turn a powdery blue-gray (as in photo). Male lower appendages bent inward at tips (a). The female's ovipositor reaches the tip of the abdomen. Wings typically held partly spread when perching.

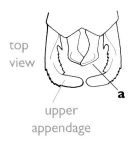

top view

a

upper appendage

Females insert eggs above the water into emergent plants like pond lily and wild iris. Eggs laid near ponds that dry up before the end of summer hatch the following spring. Larvae develop into adults in less than a month.

Distribution: C

Northern Spreadwing
Lestes disjunctus

Mature male with top of thorax black with pale blue stripes and a faint bronze luster. Abdomen dark bronze, often with a green tinge. Male lower appendages long and straight (a). In older males, the back of head, sides of thorax, and abdominal segments 1-2 and 8-10 turn a powdery blue-gray (as in photo). Female coloration lighter than in male, not turning blue-gray with age; the ovipositor does not reach the tip of the abdomen.

upper
appendage   **a**

This species was formerly known as the Common Spreadwing.

Distribution: SE, SC, SW, C

15

Taiga Bluet
Coenagrion resolutum

Similar to the Subarctic Bluet but with underside of thorax pale, and the blue at tip of abdomen does not extend onto segment 7. In male, top of thorax black with blue, usually unbroken, stripes; sides of thorax with a greenish tinge. Abdominal segment 2 with a black U-shaped mark on top.

Female similar to male or with pale areas yellowish-green to brownish, top of abdominal segments 9-10 mostly black.

Within their range Taiga Bluets inhabit almost any small permanent or temporary body of standing water.

Distribution: C

Subarctic Bluet
Coenagrion interrogatum

Similar to Taiga Bluet but with conspicuous black markings under thorax, and the blue at tip of abdomen extends onto segment 7. Top of thorax black with a blue stripe that is often divided resembling an exclamation mark (as in photo). Pale areas of thorax and abdomen blue in male, blue or greenish in female.

Female abdominal segments 9-10 mostly blue, a black spot on top of segment 9.

Like the Subarctic Darner, this damselfly is found near wetlands dominated by floating mosses.

Distribution: C

Boreal Bluet
Enallagma boreale

♂

♀

Identical in appearance to the Northern Bluet. Male blue with black markings; female light blue to yellow-green or light brown with black markings (inset). Male Boreal and Northern bluets are distinguished by the shape of their terminal appendages. Try examining the upper appendages in side view with a 16X hand lens.

Female Boreal and Northern Bluets cannot be reliably distinguished in the field unless captured when in tandem with a male.

Distribution: SE, SC, SW, C

Boreal Bluet

upper appendage

lower appendage

Northern Bluet

side view   top view

18

Northern Bluet
Enallagma cyathigerum

Male and female coloration identical to that of Boreal Bluet.
Males of the two species distinguished by the upper appendages
(See illustration on facing page).

To avoid male harassment, females will descend underwater
up to one meter deep to lay their eggs and we have seen them
remain submerged for up to 45 minutes.

Distribution: SE, SC, SW, W, C

Sedge Sprite
Nehalennia irene

Our smallest damselfly at 27 mm long. Top of thorax and abdomen metallic green in both sexes. Male abdomen with a blue tip; abdominal segments 8 and 9 of female tipped with blue.

A weak flyer. Rarely ventures over open water, preferring to fly among the stems of emergent plants and shoreline vegetation.

Distribution: C

The Emeralds (Family: Corduliidae)

Striking emerald-green eyes and a metallic green body give these dragonflies their common name. Indeed, *Somatochlora*, the genus to which most of our Emerald species belong, translates to "green-bodied." The body may also be touched with bronze, and the eyes of juveniles are red. These medium-sized dragonflies (45 to 52 mm in length) are secretive and sometimes rare inhabitants of fens, bogs, and lakes. Adults spend most of their time on the wing in search of prey.

Identification to species is challenging, requiring examination of the male terminal appendages and female vulvar lamina with a 10X hand lens. However, it's easy to narrow one's choice down to two or three species by looking for white rings on the abdomen or brown spots on the hind wings where they attach to the body. (Do not confuse these spots with the  membranule, a white and brown part of the wing in this area. See Whitehouse's Emerald on page 25).

If you catch an emerald that doesn't quite fit the descriptions in this guide, it may be one of four species that likely occur in Alaska, but have yet to be collected here: Ocellated Emerald *(Somatochlora minor)*, Brush-tipped Emerald *(Somatochlora walshii)*, Kennedy's Emerald *(Somatochlora kennedyi)*, and Muskeg Emerald *(Somatochlora septentrionalis)*. Check out the Royal British Columbia Museum guide *Introducing the Dragonflies of British Columbia and the Yukon* by Robert Cannings for photographs and descriptions of these species.

American Emerald
Cordulia shurtleffii

The only male emerald with a forked lower appendage (a).

Female appendages short (≤ 2.5 mm long) (b), vulvar lamina deeply bilobed (c).

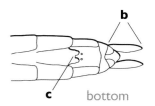

Males chase other dragonflies while patrolling defended areas. Egg laying involves dipping the tip of the abdomen in water while hovering among the stems of emergent vegetation.

Distribution: SE, SC, SW, C

Mountain Emerald
Somatochlora semicircularis

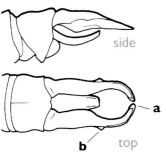

Male upper appendages viewed from above smoothly curved inward, the tips nearly touching (a); lateral tubercles conspicuously visible (b).

Female vulvar lamina notched (c), about half as long as the underside of segment 9.

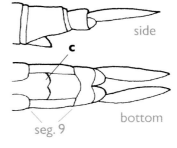

Distribution: SE, C

Delicate Emerald
Somatochlora franklini

A brown spot (a) at the base of each hind wing.

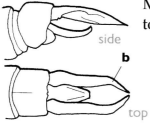

Male upper appendages bend inward towards tips (b).

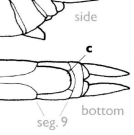

Female vulvar lamina at least as long as underside of segment 9, scoop-shaped and with a rounded tip (c).

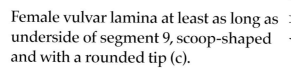

Relatively short wings and a long slender abdomen give this emerald a delicate appearance.

Distribution: SE, C

Whitehouse's Emerald
Somatochlora whitehousei

A brown spot (a) at the base of each hind wing (not to be confused with the membranule (b).

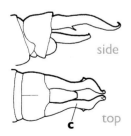

Male upper appendages viewed from above curve inward and then outward before converging at the tips (c).

Female vulvar lamina without a notch or slightly notched (d), one-half to two-thirds as long as the underside of segment 9, and projecting downward in side view (e).

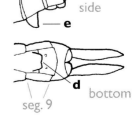

Distribution: SE

Ringed Emerald
Somatochlora albicincta

Similar to the Hudsonian Emerald. A white ring on each abdominal segment.

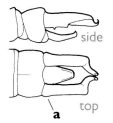

Male upper appendages viewed from above with a rounded knob at the base (a). This knob is pointed in Hudsonian Emeralds.

Female vulvar lamina deeply bilobed (b) and nearly half as long as segment 9; projects downward in dead specimens.

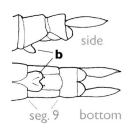

Distribution: SE, SC, SW, C

Hudsonian Emerald
Somatochlora hudsonica

Similar to the Ringed Emerald. A white ring on most abdominal segments.

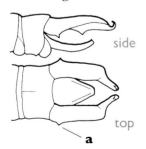

Male upper appendages viewed from above wider than segment 10; each with a pointed knob at the base (a).

Female vulvar lamina slightly notched (b), more than half as long as underside of segment 9 and projecting downward in side view.

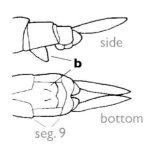

Distribution: C

Treeline Emerald
Somatochlora sahlbergi

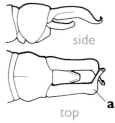

Male upper appendages viewed from above are parallel before bending sharply inward toward tips (a).

Female vulvar lamina is notched or bilobed (b); less than half as long as underside of segment 9.

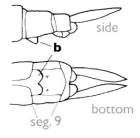

The most boreal of all dragonflies, this species prefers deep, cold ponds dominated by aquatic moss.

Distribution: W, C, N

The Blue Darners (Family Aeshnidae)

Darners, with their long, slender abdomens, were probably named for their resemblance to darning needles. Some folks believed these insects were "the Devil's darning needles," slipping into the rooms of naughty children at night to sew their lips shut. In reality, darners are harmless insects found throughout Alaska in a variety of habitats. They are strong fliers, venturing far from larval habitats to feed in backyards, parking lots, and roadways, where countless die in collisions with vehicles. We've even seen adventurous darners flying over the ocean between islands miles apart.

Darners are the largest dragonflies in Alaska (>55 mm long). They have spots on the abdomen which are blue in males and blue, green, or yellow in females. Two stripes on each side of the thorax can be blue, green, or yellow, and their shape is important in identifying species.

Male darners patrol territories and defend them from other dragonflies. After mating, females go alone to lay their eggs in vegetation or in dead wood.

Adults will prey on other dragonflies their own size. The larvae, which can be up to 40 mm long, are known to capture amphibians and even small fish. In cold, prey-limited habitats, larvae may require up to five years to transform into adults. Adults live for eight to 10 weeks.

Zigzag Darner
Aeshna sitchensis

Similar to the Azure Darner.
Front thoracic stripe bent twice,
resembling a zigzag (a). Base of
T-spot, a black marking on top of the
head, with lobes (see facing page).

Our smallest darner (< 60 mm long). Its habit of flying low and
often perching on the ground is unusual for Blue Darners.
Occurs north of the Brooks Range.

Distribution: SE, SC, C, N

Azure Darner
Aeshna septentrionalis

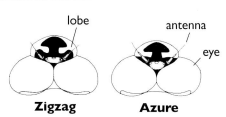

Similar to the Zigzag Darner, but with more blue on abdomen. The front thoracic stripe is bent twice (a), resembling a zigzag. T-spot, a black marking on top of the head, without lobes.

One of our smallest darners (< 61 mm long). Ranges north of the arctic treeline.

lobe

antenna

eye

Zigzag   **Azure**

Distribution: SW, C, N

Lake Darner
Aeshna eremita

Front thoracic stripe with a deep, rounded indentation (a).

Our largest darner (> 72 mm long). Will fly at 50 degrees F in light rain, but colors turn dark when cool. Often the only dragonfly flying late in the evening and even all night long during the arctic summer.

Distribution: SE, SC, SW, W, C

Subarctic Darner
Aeshna subarctica

Thoracic stripes constricted in middle giving them a bent appearance (a).

Feeds in open areas into the evening. Eggs are inserted into floating moss in bogs and fens (see photo on page 7).

Distribution: SE, SC, C

Sedge Darner
Aeshna juncea

♀

Thoracic stripes straight-sided, broad, and outlined in black (a). A pair of pale spots on the underside of each abdominal segment.

A very common darner. The common name refers to the vegetation often found in their habitat.

Distribution: SE, SC, SW, W, C

Paddle-tailed Darner
Aeshna palmata

Male upper append-
ages paddle-shaped
in side view (b).

Thoracic stripes nearly straight (a), not
outlined in black as in Sedge Darner.

Females may insert eggs into grass blades up to 1 meter above
surface of water. Adults have been known to survive a snowfall.

Distribution: SE, SC, C

Variable Darner
Aeshna interrupta

♂

As the common name implies, the lateral thoracic stripes can be variably shaped, either narrow and straight (a), or divided (i.e., interrupted) into pairs of spots.

A very common darner. Larvae can inhabit brackish waters. Will engage in feeding swarms.

Distribution: SE, SC, C, N

Skimmers (Family Libellulidae)

A dragonfly observed sitting still for more than a minute is likely a skimmer. Unlike darners and emeralds that hunt on the wing, our skimmers take a sit-and-wait approach to foraging. Most of their time is spent perched on the ground or on low vegetation between short flights to grab winged prey. Skimmers are a diverse group of dragonflies that are best described by the three genera that occur in Alaska.

The **Whitefaces** (genus *Leucorrhinia*) are small (25 to 39 mm long) black dragonflies with a white face and yellow or red markings on the abdomen; the shape, size, and number of marked segments are important for identification. When counting their abdominal segments, it's easiest to count from segment 10 (a short segment bearing the terminal appendages) towards the head.

The **King Skimmers** (genus *Libellula*) are rather fat bodied, aggressive dragonflies. We have only one species in Alaska – the easily recognized Four-spotted Skimmer.

The **Meadowhawks** (genus *Sympetrum*) are small (31 to 34 mm long) dragonflies that appear late in summer. One species is nearly all black when mature, the other a striking blood red.

Hudsonian Whiteface
Leucorrhinia hudsonica

Similar to Boreal Whiteface but smaller (< 30 mm long). In mature individuals, red spots on abdominal segments 1-7, the spot on segment 7 not reaching the end of segment. Sometimes a spot on segment 8. Juveniles have yellow spots that turn red with maturity.

Distribution: SE, SC, SW, C

Boreal Whiteface
Leucorrhinia borealis

♀

Our largest whiteface dragonfly (> 36 mm long). Male with spots on abdominal segments 1-8. Female with spots on abdominal segments 1-7, the spot on segment 7 reaching end of segment. Juveniles have yellow abdominal spots that turn red with maturity.

♂

Distribution: C, N

Belted Whiteface
Leucorrhinia proxima

juvenile ♂

Nearly identical to Crimson-ringed Whiteface. Abdominal segments 1-3 red in mature males and yellow in juveniles (see photo at left), the remaining segments black or with fine streaks on segments 4-7 (as in photos). Female with yellow or red marks on abdominal segments 1-7. Formerly called the Red-waisted Whiteface. Males will attack and subdue rival males in mid-air while their mate is laying eggs.

Distribution: SC, C

Crimson-ringed Whiteface
Leucorrhinia glacialis

Nearly identical to Belted Whiteface. Male abdominal segments 1-3 red (yellow in juveniles); thin streaks of red or yellow may be present on middle abdominal segments (4-7).

Female abdominal segments 1-7 with yellow spots, becoming red with maturity in some individuals.

Crimson-ringed   **Belted**

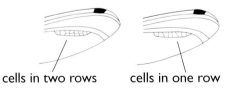

cells in two rows   cells in one row

Wing venation can be used to distinguish Belted and Crimson-ringed Whitefaces.

This species is currently known to occur in extreme southern southeastern Alaska.

Distribution: SE

Canada Whiteface
Leucorrhinia patricia

The smallest whiteface dragonfly (< 28 mm long). Male abdominal segments 1-3 red; segments 4-5 sometimes with a fine red streak. Female and juvenile male with abdominal segments 1-3 yellow, segments 4-6 with yellow spots; sometimes a fine streak on segment 7.

This diminutive whiteface was discovered outside the country of its namesake for the first time in June 2003 in both Maine and Alaska.

Distribution: C

Four-spotted Skimmer
Libellula quadrimaculata

The Four-spotted Skimmer is our most recognizable dragonfly. The common name refers to four spots on the leading edge (middle) of each wing. Also has large triangular spots at the base of each hind wing. Abdomen broad and flattened; front half yellow and rear half black. Length 43 mm.

One of the first dragonflies to emerge in spring. Males hover near ovipositing females, chasing away other dragonflies that get too close.

The Four-spotted Skimmer dragonfly was chosen as Alaska's official state insect from a vote taken by students from every public school in the state during the 1993-94 school year. As the students from Aniak pointed out: "Dragonflies eat mosquitoes, one of the state's most annoying pests."

Distribution: SE, C

Black Meadowhawk
Sympetrum danae

Mature males almost completely black with a dark face. Females and juvenile males black with a light yellow face, sides of thorax with two large yellow spots and top of abdominal segments with paired yellow spots that sometimes converge to form a stripe in females (see photo at left). In both sexes yellow gradually changes to brown and then black with maturity.

A tame little dragonfly that emerges late in the summer. *Sympetrum* means "with (or on) the rocks" and likely refers to this species' habit of frequently landing on the ground.

Distribution: SE, SC, SW, C

Cherry-faced Meadowhawk
Sympetrum internum

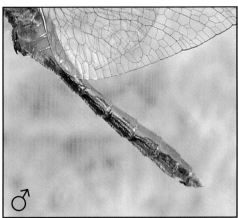

In mature individuals, face red and body mostly red. Face and body of juveniles yellow-brown. No marks on thorax. Abdomen with a jagged black stripe on sides (left).

Females drop eggs onto moist ground while hovering in tandem or while male is perched nearby.

Distribution: C

Occasional Visitors

Common Green Darner
Anax junius
The forehead has a black spot surrounded by a blue ring, and the thorax is green. A dark stripe runs the length of the abdomen, which is reddish in juveniles, turning blue in mature males and blue, gray-green, or violet in females. Some populations are migratory, and individuals occasionally venture far north of their normal range in southern Canada. Although this darner was collected near Sitka and Eagle in the 1800s, it probably does not breed here. Length: 75 mm.

Spot-winged Glider
Pantala hymenaea
A brown spot at the base of each hind wing and a propensity to soar long distances gives this dragonfly its common name. In August of 2004, Spot-winged Gliders were seen in Juneau, hundreds of miles north of their breeding range. The region's warmest summer on record likely helped these long-distance fliers reach Alaska. Length: 45-50 mm.

Pacific Spiketail
Cordulegaster dorsalis
This large (75-80 mm long) bold-colored dragonfly has aqua-blue eyes and yellow stripes and spots on a black body. Its preferred habitat is slow and warm streams draining lakes or heated by thermal springs. The first and last record of this species in Alaska was reported by Russian Explorers near Sitka in the early 1800s.

Catching and Photographing Dragonflies

More than 43 percent of Alaska's 403 million acres are considered wetlands. This is in contrast to the rest of the continental United States, where remaining wetlands make up little more than five percent of the land surface. Within Alaska's wetlands are innumerable ponds, lakes and freshwater marshes where dragonflies can breed. However, little is known about the habitat requirements, ecology, and geographic distribution of dragonflies in the state.

We hope this guide will stimulate interest in these fascinating insects and provide a starting point to learn more about them in Alaska. Anyone armed with a net, a hand lens, and a means to document what they have caught, such as a camera, can contribute to our knowledge.

Catching and Handling

Catching dragonflies can be a challenge but with practice one can become quite good at it. We like nets with about an 18-inch opening and a six-foot-long handle. The collapsible nets and handles sold by various scientific supply houses are easy to pack around and use. Once you have caught a dragonfly you can gently pinch the wings together with your thumb and forefinger and then bring it out of the net for closer examination.

Photography

Many dragonfly species in Alaska can be identified from photographs. One trick that makes photography easier is to carefully insert the dragonfly into a plastic envelope and put it into a small portable cooler with a reusable cold pack. Once cooled down the dragonfly can be "posed" on the perch of your choice. Photograph emeralds from the back paying particular attention to the terminal appendages. Photograph darners from the side paying particular attention to their thoracic side stripes. Photograph whitefaces, king skimmers, and meadowhawks from the back paying particular attention to their abdominal segments and wings.

Damselflies are much harder to photograph because they warm up very quickly and fly away, so it is important to have the camera ready and pre-focused before posing a damselfly.

Index to Species

Acknowledgements

Special thanks to Robert A. Cannings and the Royal British Columbia Museum for allowing us to use the detailed line drawings from the book "Dragonflies of British Columbia and the Yukon." This book was also indispensable to us in identifying the dragonflies we caught.

We are especially grateful to Dennis Paulson for his helpful review of our book and for verification of specimens. The key to dragonflies of Alaska by Dennis Paulson also helped us a great deal.

Kim Frangos and Pauline Strong provided considerable support and help on our many collecting trips. Marge Hermans edited and helped design the book. Mary Rabe and Karla Hart of the Alaska Department of Fish and Game's Nongame Program gave us considerable encouragement and helped make the book a reality. Jim Kruse kindly loaned us specimens from the Museum of the North, University of Alaska, Fairbanks.